Administrative Professionals Handbook

42 Ways to Bring Out the Best in Yourself and Others

Administrative Professionals Handbook

42 Ways to Bring Out the Best in Yourself and Others

by Linda Kephart Flynn

SkillPath Publications

Editor: Bill Cowles

Layout and cover design: Jason Sprenger

ISBN: 978-1-929874-99-6

10 9 8 7 6 5   11

Printed in the United States of America

Table of Contents

Introduction

Have you ever wondered why some people seem to have all the luck? How this person or that manages to attract a good job, a decent spouse and dear friends? And then there are others who never seem to get a break? In many ways, I think it boils down to a series of important character traits that translate into this: The ability to bring out the best in yourself and others. Put another way, the people with the skills and talent for maximizing their own potential and encouraging others to do the same are the ones who will generate the most "luck" in their lives.

My friend Barbara is a good example. She was hired by a Houston-based oil and gas company back in the early 1980s. Armed with her newly minted degree from the University of Texas (a double major in Spanish and philosophy), she was given the job as assistant to one of the corporate senior VPs and was seated at a desk outside the man's door. Barbara shared the executive floor's hallowed hall with two other women in similar positions, neither of whom spoke to her for the first several weeks of her job.

Barbara might have assumed their attitude of superiority, snubbing them and everyone else, if she hadn't been such a strong individual in her own right. Instead, every morning she made a point of warmly greeting them. When she had a question about the company or its protocol, she asked one of them to help her out. She even brought them treats when she'd go out on errands for her boss. She was relentless in her courting of everyone with whom she came into contact. Needless to say, Barbara's skills were quickly recognized. Other people noticed her genuine friendliness and efficient, yet gentle, organizational qualities. This reflected well on her boss, who consistently rewarded her with the company's maximum allowable raises. When the CEO needed an assistant, she was asked to move into that role down the hall. Within three years, the marketing vice president had lured her into his department, which she eventually ran.

Although Barbara has done well in her career, she's really no smarter than you or me. What she does have, however, is plenty of savvy. She figured out how to showcase her talents, how to draw people in and how to bring out the best in herself and others. Without her positive attitude, Barbara figures she would have given up long ago. "Everyone has a certain amount of nonsense they have to deal with in their careers," she says now. "It's how you perceive yourself in relation to it that matters. You can't let others determine how you see yourself or how you go about the business of your life."

People like Barbara can be an inspiration to all of us, whether we work in an office or a classroom or outdoors. For me, one of Barbara's co-workers in the marketing department, it was amazing to watch her work. She was positively relentless and relentlessly positive. Her attitude made her a joy to be with—and it made all of us work harder and smarter.

In this book, we'll examine how women like Barbara manage to make themselves look good while they're helping others to shine. We'll look at what's necessary to build and strengthen your "people" skills, how to put yourself first while you're thinking of others and how to get more done in less time. And we'll explore what it means to be the best you can be—in your career and in your life. After all, you can be a person of high quality no matter what your job, whether you're selling concessions at the baseball stadium, teaching first graders to read or running an international finance company.

The bottom line is that *you* handle your own quality control. You can mope around and feel sorry for yourself, or you can take steps to figure out your future. You can tear yourself down with nagging and negative self-talk, or you can give yourself a break and resolve to improve in the future. You can whine about having too much to do, or you can lay out a plan to prioritize and proceed. It really is all up to you.

This book may seem like it covers a lot of ground—and, indeed, it does. But it's meant to be a workbook of sorts, a place for you to start thinking about what it means to do and be your best and to offer you some suggestions for getting there. The ideas are based on the experiences of a multitude of successful people who've learned how to move through fear and anxiety into optimism and productivity. We've talked to counselors and coaches and lots of real people, and we've studied numerous volumes on everything from time management to job security. While you may want to read it straight through, we bet you'll get more from picking and choosing a few things to try. Then repeat the process with other strategies throughout the book.

Join us on this journey that will lead you down the path to giving it all you've got.

Linda

— *Linda Kephart Flynn*

Chapter 1:
How You Think

Jenna is a chronic worrier. She agonizes over everything from her job to her friends to her family. Maybe she offended someone. Perhaps she'd be unable to speak out at the meeting. Maybe her son would contract something from his annual booster shot. No matter what's going on in her life, Jenna finds a way to worry about it. As a result, Jenna's life is filled with energy-draining negativity. Getting up in the morning is difficult, because she's certain there will be another crisis.

Jenna's life is not worse than the average person's. But she's turned it into a series of catastrophes simply because she's more adept at viewing things as harmful and fearful. Jenna's pessimistic outlook has made her life miserable.

What do you think about? Do you spend your time ruminating on past failures or future fears? Do you agonize over some perceived personality deficit or feel easily slighted? If so, then you may not be getting what you want out of life. Studies show that, in large part, you create your own reality by how you think about your situation.

Of course, your thoughts are paramount when it comes to bringing out the best in yourself. You've got to get your head in the game if you ever hope to win it. If your mind isn't there, then you won't be either.

How do you align your mind with your goals? It's not that hard, if you remember that YOU are in charge of your mind. YOU can tell yourself whatever you want, for good or bad. Tell yourself enough and you may start to believe it.

There are some things you can do to get your brain on the right track. Here are just a few:

"Real success is finding your lifework in the work that you love."

— *David McCullough*

Find a Job You Love
(and Then Find a Cure for Cancer)

Although it's easy to say, locating a job you love can be a huge challenge. Just landing any job can be daunting if you're fresh out of school or trying to make a career switch or if your skills are rusty. But those who are most adept in bringing out the best in themselves say that this is crucial.

How do you find a job you love? Scores of books are available on seeking employment, as are lots of career counselors and job-search Web sites. Most of them urge you to assess yourself (in a journal perhaps) in terms of your personal vision, goals, interests and abilities. Then make a list of your:

- Top three personal interests

- Top three core values

- Top three natural abilities

- Top three acquired skills

Once you've thought about where you'd best find your perfect job, make sure your resumé sings. Then send it out or post it as much as possible. Do your research, and listen to your inner voice when you actually get called in for an interview.

"Never continue in a job you don't enjoy. If you're happy in what you're doing, you'll like yourself, you'll have inner peace. And if you have that, along with physical health, you will have had more success than you could possibly have imagined."

— Johnny Carson

Just remember, too, that the perfect job today may not be the perfect job tomorrow. You'll age and change and so will your company. So make a commitment to yourself that when you can't name something you like about your job, you'll start looking for something else.

If you wake up on Monday morning thinking, "Oh no. I have to go to work," then you'll never be able to walk cheerfully into the office with personal growth on your mind.

Right now, try to write down three things you like about your current job:

1. _____

_____

2. _____

_____

3. _____

_____

In his book *How to Be the Employee Your Company Can't Live Without*, author Glenn Shepard says, "If you can't name three, then name two. If you can't name two, name one. If you can't name one, resign immediately. You can't be passionate about your job if you can't name one thing you like about it, and you can't be good at it if you can't be passionate. You're not doing anybody any favors by staying at a job you can't be good at doing."

"Sometimes I've believed as many as six impossible things before breakfast."

— Lewis Carroll

Be Relentlessly Positive (and Positively Relentless)

Of course, you can be your best even in a job you don't love and, in fact, there's the bigger statement about your own personality. If, on the days you want to put your head down on your desk and weep, you instead keep your chin up and your eyes open, you'll find something of benefit in every situation.

Katie is a prime example. During her last year in college, she took a part-time secretarial job at a law firm to make some extra money. She was a biology major, and the lawyers never let her forget that she had no future at the firm. More than that, they treated her as though she had no future at all, except as a lowly go-fer. Nevertheless, Katie kept her wits about her and did her job without complaint. It's true, there really was no future for her at the law firm, but a client noticed Katie's willingness and efficiency at a meeting one morning. He struck up a conversation with her and ended up hiring her—as a scientist at his medical research facility.

"Human beings, by changing the inner attitudes of their minds, can change the outer aspects of their lives."

— William James

How can you stay positive? Experts point to these directions:

- **Don't do pity parties.** No matter how many people complain about their jobs, their bosses or the company, don't join in. It's bad for your career and bad for your state of mind.

- **Avoid negative people.** These folks can be like poison, with their toxicity bringing down your otherwise healthy outlook. You may not be able to avoid these types entirely, but keep your distance as much as possible.

- **Don't watch too much TV or play too many computer games.** While it's tempting to veg out in front of a tube (TV *or* computer), what starts out as 10 minutes of relaxation can easily morph into an evening of wasted opportunity.

- **Spend time with your friends and family.** It's amazing how positively distracting and inspiring loved ones can be, especially children. If you don't have any kids, find a niece or nephew to take to the park.

- **Read something motivational every day.** Find the motivational or spiritual section in the library and work your way through it. Some people find motivation in the Bible, others in the works of authors like Robert Schuler or Zig Ziglar.

- **Take an hour each day to become an expert.** What's an hour if you can learn something new that will advance you in your field? One hour a day adds up to seven hours a week, which can amount to an impressive boost in knowledge.

- **Try new things.** Experiment with things you've always wanted to do: Try hot air ballooning, for example, or cooking Asian cuisine or painting with watercolors. Trying new things will keep you energized, alert and engaged.

- **Stay active through exercise.** Countless experts will tell you that you'll feel better if you get out and exercise. So, even when you don't want to, get up and get going.

- **Reward yourself.** Set some achievable goals and then be good to yourself when you reach them. Success breeds success and helps you to stay positive.

> *"In order that people may be happy in their work, these three things are needed: They must be fit for it. They must not do too much of it. And they must have a sense of success in it."*
>
> — *John Ruskin*

Eliminate Negative Self-talk (Yes, You Can)

Imagine it's a beautiful Monday morning when one of your co-workers walks up to your desk. You smile up at her, but instead of returning your smile, she says, "You jerk. Why can't you get anything right?" How would you feel? What would you do? My guess is that you'd probably be pretty angry and vow to give that person the cold shoulder—or worse.

Now imagine that you're the one saying that to yourself. In fact, that may not be so difficult to imagine, because many of us spend lots of time talking that way to ourselves, whether we admit it or not. "Why can't I be as pretty as Jessica?" "I'm not smart enough for that" or "I know they just don't like me" are the kinds of statements that go through everyone's mind at some point.

This self-critical voice stays very busy. It remembers our failures, ignores good things that happen, sets impossible standards, assumes others view us negatively and calls us names. Not exactly someone we'd like to have around, and yet here we are, stuck with ourselves!

Believe it or not, negative thoughts serve a purpose. If you're anxious about trying something new and your inner voice tells you, "I can't do that. I'm an idiot to even think of it," then you are likely to listen and not try. Sure enough, you've relieved your own anxiety. But you've also avoided the positive feelings that would have been your reward had you actually stuck your neck out.

Once you become aware of how your self-talk sounds, imagine what a kind, supportive voice would say. Picture someone actually encouraging you. This could be a coach, a favorite teacher or a trusted friend. Replace what you say to yourself with what they would say. They're so much nicer, aren't they? Choose to listen to them.

Some people call these positive self-statements "affirmations." Whatever you name them, it helps to have a way to tell yourself about your own unique worth.

Instead of this ...	Say this ...
I'm no good	I'm a decent person
I deserve what I get	I deserve to feel good
I'm afraid	I feel confident and safe
I don't matter	I can make a difference
I'm too scared to try that	I am brave enough to take healthy risks
I can't handle mistakes	I'll manage when something goes wrong
I'm a fool	I'm a good person, mistakes and all

"The self is not something ready-made, but something in continuous formation through choice of action."

— *John Dewey*

Try New Things (Even When It's Uncomfortable)

Your inner voice may scream for you to stop, but it's often good to get outside your comfort zone. In fact, how will you learn and grow and move ahead in your life if you sit quietly in one place?

When it comes to this subject, author Sherrie Gong Taguchi offers a modification of the famous 80/20 rule in her book *The Career Troubleshooter.* "Take on roles that 80 percent of the time allow you to draw on strengths, prior experience and core skills. The other 20 percent of your efforts should take you out of your comfort zone. They should be a stretch for you. This means taking on challenges and trying your hand at responsibilities, activities and skills that are not part of your normal experience. These challenges will have a steep learning curve. Attempting them may make you feel incompetent. But putting out the effort to get better or to actually master them will add to your repertoire of capabilities and give you a strong sense of achievement."

At the time, Melinda hadn't heard of this new take on the 80/20 rule, but she was brave enough to try something new. Melinda was a writer at a small publishing company in Seattle. She did her job well, turning out stories on small businesses and helping to put the business magazine together each month. One day, her editor told her that he was supposed to give a speech at a local Rotary lunch, but had a conflict and couldn't do it. Would she go in his place? Melinda's inner critic went right to work, reminding her that she was too shy, her voice too tiny, her thoughts not important enough for the business people at the Rotary meeting. But she also didn't want to disappoint her boss, so Melinda gave it a try. She prepared well and did great and was asked back twice in the next two years. Melinda also took over as editor of a sister publication, largely because she'd proven she could get outside her comfort zone.

> *"Success is the ability to go from one failure to another with no loss of enthusiasm."*
>
> — *Sir Winston Churchill*

What will it take you to stretch? Try these suggestions:

- Call someone who's an expert at something you'd like to know about
- Make a lunch date with someone you admire
- Volunteer to write a report you wouldn't normally write
- Take on a project nobody else wants
- Offer to plan the departmental meeting
- As the saying goes, "Never be afraid to try something new. Remember, amateurs built the ark; professionals built the Titanic."

Find a Passion (and We're Not Talking About Mr. Right)

Passion about your job is a wonderful ideal. But you shouldn't stop there. Experts say that if you're not passionate about something outside of work, then you won't be passionate about your work either.

Maybe you have an interest in gardening. Why not join a local gardening group or sign up for a summer garden tour or take a class in growing herbs? Perhaps you've always wanted to learn more about cooking. Make a commitment to try a new recipe every week or sign up for a class at your local university. Maybe your love of reading could extend to joining a book group or tutoring slow readers or offering to read to classes at your local grade school. You can find all sorts of ways to take an interest and turn it into a passion.

"My passions were all gathered together like fingers that made a fist. Drive is considered aggression today; I knew it then as purpose."

— Bette Davis

Of course, it's possible you don't know what your passion might be. Here are some ways to evaluate yourself to determine interests that may become passions:

Are you …	
an extrovert	or an introvert?
Then you might try …	
ballroom dancing	gardening
volunteer work	cooking
joining Toastmasters	joining a chess club
Do you like …	
to meet new people	or prefer to stick with old friends?
Then you might try …	
joining a charity organization	entertaining at your home
organizing a dinner club	playing volleyball at the park
finding a bicycling group	girls-only getaways
Do you …	
enjoy physical activity	or are you more sedentary?
Then you might try …	
finding a hiking group	joining a quilting group
making a commitment to exercise	reading a new book every week
rock climbing	learning how to knit
Do you like …	
the arts	or the sciences?
Then you might try …	
taking dance lessons	leading groups on nature hikes
attending a jazz festival	forming an inventors' group
learning to paint	helping kids learn about bugs
Do you enjoy …	
children	or adults?
Then you might try …	
coaching a sports team	helping your elderly neighbors
leading a scout troop	joining an historic preservation group
tutoring kids in reading	hosting neighborhood parties

Are you ...	
a collector	or a tosser?
Then you might try ...	
antiquing for silver spoons	helping your friends get organized
learning about shopping Web sites	learning about selling Web sites
studying 1950s fashions	organizing a clothes exchange
Are you ...	
highly focused	or easily distracted?
Then you might try ...	
collecting rare butterfly species	daily walks in your neighborhood
reading the classics	writing haiku
learning to play the banjo	volunteering at the animal shelter

The point is that there are so many possibilities for passion. You can't force it, but if you sample enough new things, you have a greater chance of finding something that knocks your socks off. You may meet new people, too, which can have a wonderful effect on your life.

"A discovery is said to be an accident meeting a prepared mind."

— Albert von Szent-Gyorgyi

Don't Be a Victim (No More "Why Me's?")

Everyone experiences feelings of powerlessness at times in their life, but you don't have to be a victim because of it.

Instead of whining about not being asked to lunch by the gals down the hall, why not ask them first? Instead of worrying about why you were passed over for a recent promotion, why not schedule an appointment with your supervisor to get some pointers for the next time? Instead of agreeing to do every demeaning task for the co-worker who can't ever seem to manage her own work, why not devise a few nice ways of saying "no"?

In their book, *Driving the Career Highway*, authors Janice Reals Ellig and William J. Morin offer this contract, which will keep you off the victim treadmill. Don't just read it and think you'll try it some other time. If you have trouble with feeling like a victim, fill it out and sign it, too.

I, _____ , hereby proclaim that I am not a victim and that I am in control of my own destiny. I further pledge and agree:

1. that I will not allow others, such as _____ , to make decisions for me;

2. that I will not allow situations of the past, like the following, _____
_____
_____ , to repeat themselves;

3. that I will not allow myself to feel inadequate or bullied as I did in the following situations: _____
_____
_____

4. that I will accept responsibility for my own well-being as I did in the past, as in the following situations: _____
_____
_____

5) that I will again take control as I did in the past, as in the following situations: _____
_____
_____

[signed] _____

> "Time is the coin of your life. It is the only coin you have, and only you can determine how it will be spent. Be careful lest you let other people spend it for you."
>
> — Carl Sandburg

Assess Your Life (What Do You Want Now?)

When she was a teenager, Leslie heard about a movie called *Seven Up*, where 14 children from diverse backgrounds all over England were asked about their lives. Renowned director Michael Apted then revisited the kids seven years later and, as it turned out, every seven years since then. To Leslie (and millions of others) it was a fascinating project because it was a way to examine the progression of these lives and to see what kind of effect their expectations and experiences had on the reality of what eventually happened to them (*49 Up* came out in 2005).

Leslie became so interested in the Up Series, in fact, that she launched a similar device in her own life: Every year, as her birthday approaches, Leslie gets out her list of life goals and reexamines what she's done and what she still wants to do. Then she sets up her video camera and records herself talking about her life. On the tape (the same tape, so she has one long chronicle), she asks—and answers—questions such as "What's the best thing I accomplished this past year?" or "What would I change about this year?" or "What are my goals for the next year?" Then she watches the tape on New Year's Day, about six months after her birthday.

For Leslie it's been a wonderful way to assess her life's path and, she believes, keep her headed in the right direction. "Life's so short," she says. "This helps me to get the most out of every day."

"The person who makes a success of living is the one who sees his goal steadily and aims for it unswervingly. That is dedication."

— Cecil B. deMille

There are plenty of ways to track what you want in your life, but it's important to make those assessments on a regular basis. You might start by weighing what areas you most want to nurture now.

How much of your life do you want to allot to:

_____% Family		_____% Hobbies
_____% Friendships		_____% Travel
_____% Education		_____% Volunteering
_____% Work		_____% Reading
_____% Love life		_____% Relaxing/sleeping
_____% Health/exercise		_____% Other
_____% Religion/spirituality		

100% | **Total**

You might also want to develop a Monster To-do list. This is not your normal "update my resumé" catalog of things you want to get done, but rather a record of things you'd like to accomplish in your lifetime that you haven't done yet. This is a list where you dream big without worrying whether or not the dreams are realistic. Then pick one goal and take action. For example, this is my list:

1. Write children's books
2. Sail around the Greek Islands
3. Plant a huge garden
4. Relearn the piano pieces I played in my last recital (at age 13)
5. Do yoga every day
6. Learn to speak Italian
7. Set up a stained glass studio
8. Take a cooking class
9. Live in Venice for a year
10. Join the choir at church
11. Hike the Pacific Crest Trail
12. Learn how to rollerblade
13. Take a watercolor class
14. Own a dog
15. Take my kids to Disney World
16. Try a new recipe every week
17. Get a trampoline and jump on it every day
18. Go up in a hot air balloon
19. Learn how to sell stuff on eBay®
20. Act in a movie

Some are easy; some not so. I think I can cross off number 15 this year and maybe number 10. And I'm working on numbers 1 and 16. So even though there are things that I may never do (number 9, for example) there are others that are certainly attainable. And, doggone it, number 9 will be on my list forever!

Keep the list somewhere where you can glance at it from time to time, make changes or even cross things off. You'll find it a valuable way to look forward in a powerfully optimistic way.

> *"Plans are only good intentions unless they immediately degenerate into hard work."*
>
> — *Peter Drucker*

Learn From Your Past
(and Try Not to Repeat Your Mistakes)

Some people believe that, without some self-examination, we keep making the same mistakes over and over and over again, unless we finally realize what we're doing wrong and take steps to change. There's some truth to this, if you consider people who leave jobs they deem "boring" only to find another one that's equally "boring;" or people who have multiple marriages with the same type of person. Or even those who need to move a lot but don't realize that they just keep landing in the same kind of town.

If you find yourself in similar situations, then it's time to learn from your mistakes so that you can stop the cycle. "An important step before making a significant life change," say Karen Dowd and Sherrie Gong Taguchi in their book *The Ultimate Guide to Getting the Career You Want*, "is to review your life experiences to date, understanding your accomplishments and missteps thoroughly, analyzing your experience to discover patterns and trends, and bringing your learnings from the past to bear on the choices you have and the decisions you are making in the present."

How can you do that? Start by examining your experiences. Look for patterns that may be relevant. Dowd and Taguchi suggest asking questions like these:

- What are some recent life or career changes that you've made and what motivated these changes (e.g., money, dissatisfaction, opportunity or age)? How satisfied were you with the outcome and why?

- How did you make these decisions (e.g., with help from others, impulsively, or after careful research)? How satisfied were you with the outcome and why?

- What information/resources have you used when you have been faced with a change in your life or career (friends, newspapers, professional associations, the Internet or other sources)? How satisfied were you with the outcome and why?

- What are two or three key behaviors (e.g., work ethic) and attitudes (e.g., helpful to others) that may have helped your career and your life progress over the years?
- What are two or three key behaviors (e.g., lack of emotional control) or attitudes (e.g., perceived arrogance) that may have hindered your career or life progress over the years?
- Which situations were difficult for you? How did you handle them? What did you learn from them? What, if anything, did you change about yourself as a result of these experiences?
- What are some of your major sources of satisfaction and some of your major frustrations?
- What have you learned so far about managing your life and career? What are some of the lessons learned that you would like to take into consideration as you explore your "what's next?"
- If you had it to do all over again, what would you do differently?

> *"Believe in yourself! Have faith in your abilities! Without a humble but reasonable confidence in your own powers you cannot be successful or happy."*
>
> *— Norman Vincent Peale*

Chapter 2:
How You Look

It may seem shallow, but *looking* your best actually has an effect on *doing* your best. And it's important to remember that it's not just how other people perceive you either. Looking your best comes from within and can help you radiate a sense of calm and self-possession.

Most everyone has experienced that feeling of knowing they're well put together. The blouse is perfectly pressed; the skirt is just the right length and color. The shoes and jewelry match beautifully and everything flows just right. Wouldn't it be great if you could feel like that every day? Well, it's certainly worth a try!

"I was always looking outside myself for strength and confidence, but it comes from within. It is there all the time."

— Anna Freud

Take Care of Your Body (and It'll Take Care of You)

The number one thing you can do to bring out the best in yourself is to treat your body well. Everybody knows that if you look good, you feel good, right? And the best way to look good is to keep yourself hale and healthy.

First off—and maybe most important—don't smoke. Even if you never exercise and eat only junk food, saying "no" to tobacco will keep you alive longer. In addition, that one action will keep you looking young longer and give you more stamina and energy over the course of your lifetime. If you've already started the nicotine habit, make a date with yourself to quit. And then do it.

Of course, diet and exercise are important too. Sara is a good example of the difference these two priorities can make. As a young graduate student, Sara was given the opportunity to work as an assistant on an outreach grant through the University of Minnesota. Her job required extensive travel throughout the state, speaking to and working with schoolchildren. A lifelong believer in the benefits of a healthy diet and exercise, Sara took her regimen on the road, never missing a day on the treadmill or track, rarely succumbing to a quick burger or fries. Today, Sara runs a bigger grant program, raises two small children and continues her commitment to a healthy lifestyle. "I couldn't do all I do if I didn't make time to exercise," she says. "And I simply feel better eating healthfully. Why wouldn't I do what makes me feel right?"

"As I see it, every day you do one of two things: Build health or produce disease in yourself."

— Adelle Davis

What's a good exercise program? Recommendations are all over the board, but the important thing is that you do something. In their best-seller *You, On a Diet*, authors Mehmet C. Oz and Michael F. Roizen suggest starting an exercise program with a 30-minute walk every day. They say that 30 minutes a day can fight depression as well as anti-depressants can. "Thirty minutes of daily walking has been shown to decrease the risk of breast cancer by 30 percent and increase the rate of survival by 70 percent. Plus, it also improves the survival rates of heart attack victims by 80 percent." The great thing is that you don't have to do all of your exercise at once. Break it up into two 15-minute sessions, or even three 10-minute ones. But do something to exercise your body and the payoffs will be enormous.

What about diet? It's crucial to eat regularly and to consume enough fruit, vegetables, protein, whole grains, milk and water. If you're interested in what's recommended for your age, weight and level of physical activity, the United States Department of Agriculture has developed an intriguing Web site that allows you to customize your diet according to the food pyramid. Go to www.mypyramid.gov for suggestions on eating healthfully.

"Over the years your beliefs become walking autobiographies, telling friends and strangers alike of the minor and major stresses of your lives."

— *Marilyn Ferguson*

Dress the Part
(and the Parts Will Come to You)

Not so long ago, women's business attire was discussed with much more passion than it is now. Career gals were admonished to wear power suits that shouldn't—and yet often did—look like men's attire. Ruffles were out, sensible shoes were in. Black was the ultimate authority color, blue was for wimps. It was an era of heated discussion.

Although times have relaxed somewhat, it doesn't mean that it no longer matters what you wear. "As a business professional, you represent a brand—the brand of you," says Carmine Gallo, a Pleasanton, California-based presentation coach and author of *10 Simple Secrets of the World's Greatest Business Communicators*. "How you talk, walk, act and look reflects the brand. Before you even speak a word, most people will size you up by the way you appear. So you should seriously consider your wardrobe."

You should also consider what's appropriate where you work. If you work in a bank, you should look quietly conservative, dressed, perhaps, in slacks and a blazer. If you work for a radio station, you can probably be more relaxed—unless you're calling on advertising clients. Notice what others are wearing and try, within reason, to follow suit.

The popular movie *The Devil Wears Prada* really drove home the point when Andrea Sachs, the gangly assistant played by Anne Hathaway, finally gets some help with her wardrobe. After several weeks of being shunned by everyone ("Do you have some prior commitment? Some hideous skirt convention you have to go to?"), Andy shows up for work in an outrageously chic outfit and, suddenly, finds the other office gals—including Meryl Streep's character, the haughty editor Miranda Priestly—willing to consider her a player. Now, most of us wouldn't wear sequined tops, over-coated minidresses and knee-high boots, but it worked at the high-fashion magazine where Andy worked. Appropriate clothes could make all the difference in your workplace as well.

> *"It is only shallow people who do not judge by appearances. The true mystery of the world is the visible, not the invisible."*
>
> — *Oscar Wilde*

And it's not just style and fitting in that's important. In fact, as authors Jennifer Musselman and Patty Fletcher point out in *The Hip Girl's Handbook for the Working World*, it's probably just as crucial to be clean and tidy. "Take a close look," they advise. "Is your shirt spot-free, ironed and tucked in? Does it reek of smoke from last night's social gathering? Are your shoes shined or all scuffed up? Are your nylons snagged or sagging something fierce? Can you see your thong underwear when you bend over? Do you have any deodorant smeared on your shirt? Are your nails noticeably chipped or uneven? It's the details, after all, that set a hip girl apart from the rest. You don't just look (and smell) good; you clearly take pride in presenting your best appearance!"

When choosing your wardrobe, consider the following:

Tops

- Blouses or knits?
- Short sleeves or long?
- Collared or not?
- Buttons or pull-over?
- Solid or print?
- Tucked in or hanging out?
- Loose or form-fitting?

Shoes

- Closed toes or open?
- High heels or low?
- Straps or not?
- Neutral or bold?
- Expensive or cheap?

Accessories

- Matching purse or leather briefcase?
- Necklaces: Long or short?
- Bracelets?
- Earrings: Simple or dangly?
- Rings?

Bottoms

- Pants or skirts?
- Natural fiber or polyester?
- Long or short?
- Neutral color or print?
- Panty hose or bare legs?
- Flat-front or pleated?
- Conservative or stylish?

Hair

- Short or long?
- Coiffed or natural?
- Colored or not?
- Curled or straight?
- Bows, bands, ribbons or plain?

Of course, every day is a new decision, but if you've stocked your closet with simple items that won't go out of style tomorrow, then you'll have a much easier time when it comes to getting dressed every morning. Unless you work for a high-fashion magazine, that is.

> "In new situations, I look carefully at appearances. In familiar ones, I glance."
>
> — Mason Cooley

Dress for Your Work Environment (It's an Extension of You)

Even if you know all about making a good impression with your clothes, hair and accessories, remember that your workspace says just as much about you as does your personal appearance. Whether you like it or not, your office is an extension of your professional image.

So how do you make it work to your advantage? Consider these elements:

- **Furniture arrangement.** To create a formal atmosphere and to maintain a bit of distance from your visitors, you may want to set your desk in the middle of the floor with chairs facing it. To project a confident image, position the desk against a wall.

- **Messy desks.** A small amount of clutter actually denotes comfort and friendliness. Too much, however, may cause visitors to think you don't care about making a good impression. At the other extreme, an immaculate desk implies coldness and an insufficient workload.

- **Decorations.** Leave the stuffed animals at home. Plants and draperies suggest a more comfortable, relaxed attitude, while books and artwork express sincerity. Job-related certificates and awards reassure visitors that you are experienced and competent.

What about things that make you comfortable? Does your office exist only to impress others?

While your workspace certainly does make a statement about you, that statement doesn't have to be solely for evaluation by others. By all means, bring in a picture of your kids or that small figurine your husband gave you for your last birthday. This is where you spend your time and you should enjoy being here.

"When I enter the working environment of many people, my immediate thought is 'No wonder this person feels so stressed out,'" writes Richard Carlson, author of *Don't Sweat the Small Stuff at Work*. "You spend an enormous amount of time where you work. Why not take a tiny bit of time, energy and money and brighten it up, even a little?"

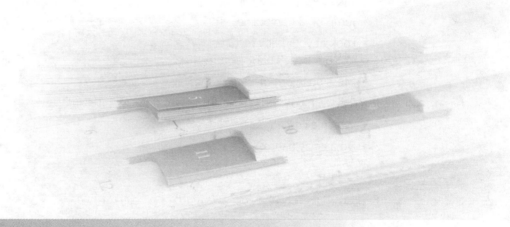

"Before you begin a thing, remind yourself that difficulties and delays quite impossible to foresee are ahead. If you could see them clearly, naturally you could do a great deal to get rid of them, but you can't. You can only see one thing clearly, and that is your goal. Form a mental vision of that and cling to it through thick and thin."

— Kathleen Norris

Smile (It's Your Best Feature)

Of course, you don't want to walk around with a silly grin on your face all the time, but a sincere smile tells people that you're approachable and at ease with yourself. Moreover, a smile will actually lift your mood, according to several studies. When you smile, they say, you feel better about yourself and the world.

How do you get yourself to smile? Try these ideas:

- Smile at yourself in the mirror
- Tell a joke
- Hug someone you love
- Bake cookies
- Take a walk in the rain
- Jump on a trampoline
- Look at your baby pictures (or your baby's baby pictures)
- Dress up in out-of-date clothes
- Play with your kids
- Watch a comedy show
- Do a crazy dance

Chapter 3:
How You Act

Back in the 1960s, Dr. William Glasser wrote a very popular book called *Reality Therapy*. For the layperson, its premise was that you could change your reality by changing your behavior. If you act like you love exercise, for example, then pretty soon you will.

While we're not suggesting therapy, we do believe that how you act speaks volumes to others—and to yourself—about how you view your general worth in the world. When you take concrete, actual steps to bring out the best in yourself, whether you actually buy it at first or not, then you're more likely to succeed. Your chances of being your best increase when you act as though it's a given.

> *"That which we persist in doing becomes easier, not that the task itself has become easier, but that our ability to perform it has improved."*
>
> — *Ralph Waldo Emerson*

Choose Your Friends and Associates Wisely
(It Really Is Who You Know)

At first, Bethany was happy in her new job. As the assistant to the human resources director, her job was to manage incoming resumés and schedule interviews with everyone throughout the company. She got to meet lots of new people and deal with a whole host of job-seekers nationwide, all of whom who were interested in the nationally known computer company.

About three months into the job, however, Bethany started hanging out with a group of young women who weren't so excited by their positions. Initially, it was a lunchtime friendship, then the women started going out after work. Pretty soon, Bethany found herself griping about her job right along with them. The more they complained, the worse it got. Bethany eventually left the company, even though her boss had offered to help her find a mentor who could shepherd her up the career ladder.

Did Bethany make the right choice? Probably not. When you want to get ahead, look *up* the food chain for your friends and associates, not *down*. You'll never get ahead by hanging out with malcontents. "If someone leaves a trail of conflicts with other people behind him or her, don't walk on the trail with that person," says Gini Graham Scott in *A Survival Guide for Working With Humans*. "You're likely to get stuck on that trail yourself."

Hanging with the right people can make a huge difference in your career—and not just by glomming onto folks who are three levels above you. The right people, who have good ideas, can-do attitudes and a positive outlook, will take you much farther than those who whine, complain or back-stab.

"Associate with well-mannered persons and your manners will improve. Run around with decent folk and your own decent instincts will be strengthened."

— Stanley Walker

How do you find the right people who will benefit both your career and your life? Consider these ideas:

- **Join a professional organization.** Whether you're a business communicator or a public relations specialist or an accounting administrator, there's probably a group of like-minded individuals who meet regularly in your town. Seek them out and attend their gatherings.

- **Join a committee.** Find out who's planning the company picnic or holiday party, then offer to help out. Whether it's setting the tables or handling the entertainment, there are always jobs to do.

- **Go to the gym.** Maybe your company sponsors exercise classes, has a company workout room, fields softball teams or holds an annual golf tournament. Join in and sweat with others who will likely welcome getting to know you outside the office.

- **Find a mentor.** Look around you and identify someone whose counsel you would welcome, then ask them to meet with you for 30 minutes a month. Use those 30 minutes to ask about career ideas, working strategies and anything else that would further your advancement up the ladder. Good sources of mentors include your management team, industry associations, your clergy and professors. Also consider people such as retirees, local business owners and people associated with your hobbies.

- **Have a pen pal.** When you were a kid, this was a fun way to meet people from foreign lands. These days, the internet makes it easy to correspond with those who might be considered e-mail mentors. Check professional organizations for matching services or Web sites such as www.mentors.ca/findamentor.html, or e-mail someone whose article you enjoyed

"When the character of a man is not clear to you, look at his friends."

— *Japanese proverb*

Determine What's Expected of You (and Then Just Do It)

Everyone should have a job description, even if you're an entrepreneur launching a new dog-washing business. You need to know how you're going to spend your time each and every day.

If you don't have a job description, then find out if you can write one up. Determine, from your supervisor, the human resources director and any others in the know, what your job entails, and then put it all down on paper. A good job description should include:

- The position's title
- The department
- The person to whom you directly report
- Overall responsibility
- Key areas of responsibility
- Those with whom you work on a regular basis

Once you've got it down, give your supervisor and the HR department a copy. Then make sure you fulfill the tasks included in the job description.

Go the Extra Mile
(Even if You Have to Walk)

Okay, so you know how to do your job, but what really gets you noticed? If you do even more. We're not talking about making yourself crazy, working all weekend or going against your principles, but doing more than what's expected will work wonders for your career.

When we do more than others expect, we get noticed. It's that simple. At work, this often means we'll get first crack at advancement opportunities. After all, when hiring or promoting, management generally considers employees' ability to do more than is expected. Furthermore, when we've completed our tasks, we can help others finish theirs. Not only will our boss appreciate it, but our co-workers will too, and our work environment will be more pleasant.

Tessa practiced this technique better than anyone I've ever known. When her boss asked her to plan the department meeting, she not only secured the conference room and came up with an agenda, but she also ordered muffins and summarized past meetings' goals and objectives. When her co-worker asked her to write an article for the company newsletter, Tessa offered to write two. You could even see her cheerfully busing lunchroom tables where others had left a mess.

Whether or not you want to go that far, remember that going beyond what's strictly expected of you not only displays your best side, but also easily brings out the best in others.

"If you can't have faith in what is held up to you for faith, you must find things to believe in yourself, for a life without faith in something is too narrow a space to live."

— George E. Woodberry

Don't Whine
(It's Not That Much Fun Anyway)

I just don't want to write about whining. Whining is boring. It's not what I was cut out to do. Why do I have to do this? It's just not fair! That wasn't appealing, was it? That's how we sound when we whine, although it's even worse when it's coming out of your mouth rather than appearing as words on a page. As author Larry Winget writes in *Shut Up, Stop Whining, and Get a Life*: "Your results are your own damn fault, no one cares about your problems. Get off your butt and go to work."

Whining is a habit that can be hard to break. How to stop? Try these suggestions:

- **Enlist the help of a friend.** Ask your dearest friend (or someone who spends a lot of time with you) to point out when you're whining. Then make a conscious effort to turn the whining into more positive language.

- **Keep a whining journal.** Every time you start to whine or even feel like whining, make a mental note to put it down in writing. Then you can still vent those feelings, but without subjecting anyone else to it.

- **Count your blessings.** When you're tempted to whine, turn your mind around and think about what makes you happy. Instead of complaining about making sack lunches every day, remind yourself how much money you're saving and how much healthier you're eating.

- **Figure out how to fix it.** Maybe you've got a legitimate gripe. For example, you're expected to do a job that requires extreme concentration, yet you work in a tiny, loud cubicle. Instead of whining, think about ways you can overcome this difficulty. Could you use the conference room? Work at home? Plug into your iPod® and play soothing music?

However you choose to handle it, the best course of action is to eliminate the whining altogether. I mean, really, it just doesn't sound right. You've got to stop!

> *"Politeness and consideration for others is like investing pennies and getting dollars back."*
>
> — *Thomas Sowell*

Put Together a Team
(Get a Little Help From Your Friends)

Before Denise and her husband purchased their small printing company, she was a stay-at-home mom who'd given up her career as a CPA to raise her twins. She taught yoga one afternoon a week and looked forward to the prospect of her kids starting kindergarten in the fall.

With her full-time job in their new business, though, Denise realized she needed lots of help. That was when it occurred to her that she needed a "team," both at work and at home. One by one, she found an excellent computer guy, a personal chef service, a holistic doctor who could keep her healthy and friends (like me) to have lunch with once a week. It's a supportive group that helps keep her sane and happy.

Entrepreneur or employee, having a team makes a lot of sense. Who's on your side, both at work and outside the office? Can you list those who help you get your life done? These can be your friends, colleagues or co-workers, or anyone else whom you can call on for help and support.

My personal team:

Name	Function	Relationship

Don't Procrastinate (You'll Only Regret It Later)

It's hard to bring out the best in yourself when you're putting off doing something that needs to be done. Not only does it look bad, but it usually makes you feel bad, too. And you can't be your best when you feel bad.

Why do we procrastinate? There are a whole host of reasons, from fear of failure to fear of success. Maybe the task is too difficult or the information too vague. If procrastination is a regular problem for you, then you need to figure out what's getting in your way and devise a plan to eliminate (or at least minimize) it from your life. Here are some strategies:

- **Create a productive environment.** Find a place to work with no distractions. If your desk is right in the middle of an activity hub, look for someplace to go where you can concentrate. If your workspace is too messy to lay your materials out in front of you, then clean it up before you get started. Don't fall into the trap, however, of procrastinating by creating your perfect environment. You can only do so much filing and cleaning before those activities begin to block your progress.

- **Challenge your myths.** On one side of a piece of paper, write down why you're procrastinating. On the other, try to challenge the reality of the situation as convincingly as possible. For example, you might think your research is incomplete, that you need two more days to really get enough information. The truth is, you will never collect all the information you possibly could. Better to finish your project now, with the information you have, than to keep doing research and risk not finishing at all.

- **Break it down.** Instead of doing the entire project in one sitting, divide it into smaller chunks. By doing this, the project never has a chance to take on massive proportions in your mind. Even if the project is something nebulous, such as "make new friends" you can break it down to 1) find an organization with like-minded people; 2) attend a meeting; 3) ask someone I met at the meeting to lunch; and 4) make a date for a movie. Whatever the challenge, you can always reduce it to smaller pieces.

- **Get a new attitude.** Changing our attitude toward the task, when possible, may go a long way toward keeping us from procrastinating. Tell yourself that whatever you have to do isn't so bad or difficult, that you either know how to do it, or that you can learn how while you're doing it. You may find, too, that if you start early on a particular assignment, your attitude never has a chance to get negative in the first place!

- **Get help.** If you're really determined not to procrastinate, then get help from the supportive people in your life. Once or twice a week, e-mail a progress report to a friend, relative or mentor, and declare your promise for the next few days. If you slip, despite your very good intentions, talk to someone about it. They may be able to help you put your slip into perspective and get back on track.

> *"Only the curious will learn and only the resolute overcome the obstacles to learning. The quest quotient has always excited me more than the intelligence quotient."*
>
> — *Eugene S. Wilson*

Speak Up
(Communicate Like a Pro)

Next to how you look, nothing says more about you than what comes out of your mouth. And it's not just the words you say, but how you say them, when you say them and when you say nothing at all.

Some people talk too much, while others are so quiet no one remembers they were in the room. How you strike that balance between too much and too little should come from a blend of your personality and the company you keep. "Communication is complex because it involves people and their tone, language, experiences, cultures, personalities and beliefs," says Michelle Burke, president of Executive Counterparts, a consulting company based in San Francisco, and author of *The Valuable Office Professional*. "Considering all this, it's no wonder we have miscommunications."

Burke suggests evaluating yourself to get a picture of where you rank, from strong to weak, in your visual, vocal and verbal skills. Take a good look at each area and be honest when rating yourself.

I. Visual

	Strong				Weak
Eye contact	5	4	3	2	1
Facial expression	5	4	3	2	1
Body language	5	4	3	2	1

II. Vocal

	Strong				Weak
Tone	5	4	3	2	1
Timing	5	4	3	2	1
Pauses	5	4	3	2	1

III. Verbal

	Strong				Weak
Clarity	5	4	3	2	1
Language	5	4	3	2	1
Understanding	5	4	3	2	1

To improve the areas in which you're weak, consider asking a friend or colleague to give you feedback. You might also set up a video camera and tape yourself presenting a businesslike request or giving a presentation. Get a friend or mentor to assess your performance and give suggestions for improvement.

Burke also offers these ideas for effective speaking and listening:

Tips for effective speaking

Be accountable: Accept total responsibility for your communication

Be specific: Remember—who, what, why, when

Be prepared: Create an action plan; do your homework or research

Be timely: Be sensitive to the timing and environmental "mood"

Be direct: State your desired result first, and add details later

Be aware: Know your communication strengths and weaknesses

Tips for effective listening

Be accountable: Accept responsibility for knowing and understanding what is asked of you

Ask questions: Ask for clarity to ensure that you understand the purpose and result

Be aware: Be aware of the distractions that will affect your listening, and choose not to let them get in your way

Stay focused: Focus on the communicator and on what is being said. Catch yourself when you realize your mind is wandering.

Be honest: Admit when you are not listening, and ask the speaker to repeat. If this isn't a good time to listen, let the speaker know, and set up a better time.

Be willing: Accept the consequences when you don't listen for understanding. Listen better in the future.

"Speak on, but be not overtedious."

— *William Shakespeare*

Keep Emotions in Check
(No Crying, Yelling or Rudeness)

When Sandra was first hired by a giant telecommunications company, it seemed she was on her way. Her resumé was stellar and the company was excited to get her. Her job in customer relations would be a first step in what the human resources people thought would be a long and successful career for her at the company.

But Sandra had a small problem. Every time she encountered an obstinate customer or a demanding boss or a curt co-worker, she cried. She couldn't help herself; she just teared up and, inevitably, had to excuse herself. Sandra worked at two more companies before she finally found a mentor who helped her learn some strategies for keeping her emotions under control.

On the other end of the spectrum, Carol was a stick of dynamite waiting to explode. A hard-working employee when everything was going well, Carol simply lost her temper when faced with someone who disagreed with her or otherwise thwarted her. She was snide and snippy, in a way that was a turn-off to everyone around her. Carol ran through a series of employers, usually leaving in anger before she was fired, until she finally got her realtor's license and began selling houses. Her anger, however, still gets in her way because she's never learned to master her temper.

How women behave in the workplace (or anywhere else) is judged differently than how men behave. It's a fact of life, whether you like it or not. That's why it's even more important that you keep your emotions in check. They get in your way, certainly, but you'll also be looked upon in a negative light if you don't learn to control them.

Some techniques for controlling your emotions:

1. Leave the situation physically. Sometimes it's better to excuse yourself until you can calm down.

2. Remove yourself mentally. Whenever Francine faced a difficult situation, she imagined herself perched on a light bulb over the same room, viewing the situation with detachment and aplomb.

3. Devise a code word for yourself that will help you remember you're in charge. When she felt herself starting to lose it, Daria always said "pizza pie" over and over. For some reason, the words comforted her and helped her focus.

> *"Emotions get in the way, but they don't pay me to start crying at the loss of 269 lives."*
>
> — *Ted Koppel*

Chapter 4:
How You Live

As I see it, how you act is what you do on the surface. How you live goes clear to the core. These are your beliefs, what rocks you, what makes you tick. You can bring out the best in yourself and others, in part, by how you act. But if you truly want to fulfill your potential—and help others reach theirs—then you'll have to go deeper. You'll have to be a person of high quality all the way through.

This isn't always easy, especially if you had a difficult childhood or are having a challenging adulthood. But others have surely overcome tough times, and you can too. Consider, for example, Washington Roebling, whose father, John, had a dream to build the Brooklyn Bridge more than a century ago. Although experts at the time believed it was impossible, John finally persuaded the city to support the project that only he and his son knew how to build.

Just a few months into the project, however, John died from tetanus and his son, Washington, suffered permanent brain damage from working too long in compressed air under the river. Washington couldn't speak, write or walk, but his mind was alert and he could move one finger. He was so determined to realize his father's dream that he developed a code, which made it possible to communicate with his wife Emily by tapping on her arm with his finger. Washington tapped on his wife's arm for 13 years, relaying all the instructions for the engineers. Today, the Brooklyn Bridge stands as a testament to how we can overcome any obstacle, if we want to.

Would you be so gallant and brave? What's at your core?

> *"Do the one thing you think you cannot do. Fail at it. Try again.*
> *Do better the second time. The only people who never tumble are those*
> *who never mount the high wire. This is your moment. Own it."*
>
> *—Oprah Winfrey*

Learn and Use Good Manners
(Time to Be Emily Post)

Ann was a stickler for "thank you" notes. If she sent a gift and didn't receive a "thank you," then she simply struck that person off her list. When she went out of her way for a colleague and wasn't thanked in writing, she hesitated to help again. And anyone who interviewed with her for a job was completely out of the running if they hadn't followed up with a note.

Perhaps Ann was a bit overboard on the "thank you" note thing, but people will judge you on how adept you are with the social graces—especially if those social graces were more rigid in their generation than in yours. So if you want to bring out the best in yourself and others, you'd do well to remember your manners.

> *"Gratitude is the most exquisite form of courtesy."*
>
> — *Jacques Maritain*

If you don't know proper etiquette, where can you learn? There are lots of books that have the answers, from Miss Manners to Emily Post. There are classes, such as those offered by The Etiquette Institute in Ohio, the Etiquette-Network in Illinois or the Business Training Works in Maryland (Do a Web search for "etiquette" for local companies or look in the yellow pages for classes near you). And there are a few Web sites (although most want to charge you something), such as www.etiquette.tips4me.com or www.etiquetteexpert.com.

Here are some etiquette basics:

"Thank you" notes are good. Write one after: A job interview, receiving a gift of any kind, dinner with your boss, help from a mentor. Anytime you would verbally say "Thanks," you should consider putting it in writing.

Saying "Thank you" is good, too. Whenever someone does you a favor—whether opening a door or presenting a gift—practice the art of saying "Thank you." This is a basic habit, but one that's valued at every level of society.

Be punctual. When the meeting starts at 9 a.m., be there five minutes early. When you have lunch plans for noon, make sure you're there at noon.

Keep your word. Do what you say you're going to do. If you think you may not really do something, then don't say you might. You'll only disappoint.

Stay sober. Don't overindulge in alcoholic beverages at company functions or business meals—or you may regret what happens.

Return phone calls and e-mails promptly. When someone has taken the time to call or write, it's only good manners to respond as soon as possible.

Keep your cell phone on vibrate. Whenever you're in a public place, it's best not to let your cell phone take center stage. That includes when you're talking on it: Don't indulge in "cell yell."

Obviously, there are hundreds—maybe thousands—more etiquette rules that you might want to know about. In fact, whole books have been written about e-mail manners alone. Invest in a few manuals, study up then refer to them whenever necessary.

"Good manners will open doors that the best education cannot."

— Clarence Thomas

Always Be Gracious
(It's Even More Than Being Polite)

Beyond manners, being gracious involves a deep level of kindness and courtesy, tact and delicacy. Or, as the dictionary describes it: Graciousness is characterized by charm, good taste and generosity of spirit.

It's this generosity of spirit that will serve you when you're looking to bring out the best in yourself and others. You can demonstrate this trait when you shrug off a petty criticism with a smile, when you wave and let someone else exit the parking garage first, when you cheer on your co-workers' success, even if you're secretly jealous. It's when we attempt to share our essence, or our spirit, in our daily interactions that we become most gracious.

Being gracious involves giving of yourself in ways that are quiet and confident. It means thinking of others and what they need most. It takes practice to generously and tactfully share with others what you know, to deliberately make another person feel better, to unselfishly bring joy and happiness to those who need them.

Karen learned about being gracious from her grandmother. "We had a relative who happened to be very fat," she says. "My dad, a practical joker with a unique sense of humor, would always ask my grandmother if this particular woman had lost any weight. Eventually, it became kind of a running joke, and my grandmother later told this woman that my dad always asked about her. Of course, she didn't tell her *what* he asked, just that he always asked about her. From that point on, this woman had the highest opinion of my dad, because he always asked about her."

*"I appreciate people who are civil, whether they mean it or not.
I think: Be civil. Do not cherish your opinion over my feelings. There's
a vanity to candor that isn't really worth it. Be kind."*

— Richard Greenburg

How do you learn to be gracious? Some of this may sound like Sunday school, but being gracious does come from pretty much the same place as spirituality. It's all in how you relate to others and to your higher self. Here are some suggestions:

- **Treat others the way you want to be treated.** It's the Golden Rule made secular, but every bit as important no matter how it's stated. This is the number one imperative in life and one that we must continually learn and relearn. When you're tempted to be mean or petty, think about how you would feel if someone treated you that way. When you want revenge, consider how it would hurt to be on the receiving end. Let that determine what you do.

- **Let your actions make a difference in the world.** Of course, you can't be Mahatma Gandhi and work in an office in America. But you can take small steps toward making changes in the world. Volunteer in your local soup kitchen. Offer to pick up a few groceries for your elderly neighbor. Rally your co-workers to clean up a local park. Countless ways exist to get outside yourself in a meaningful way.

- **Practice generosity.** Even if you're on a limited financial budget, you can still be generous. Whether it's sending a $5 check to the Red Cross or dropping a few extra coins in the church offering plate, the act of giving will actually give to you. In addition, generosity doesn't have to be financial. You can be generous with your time and talents, with your heart and hands.

- **Be kind.** You don't have to love everyone to be nice to them. Kindness goes beyond how one person actually *feels* about another and extends into how we treasure other people just for their humanness. That's the premise of the "random acts of kindness" movement that swept the nation. Being kind is not only good for others, but it's good for you, too.

> *"I am still determined to be cheerful and happy, in whatever situation I may be; for I have also learned from experience that the greater part of our happiness or misery depends upon our dispositions, and not upon our circumstances."*
>
> — *Martha Washington*

Keep on Learning
(Final Exams Shouldn't Be so Final)

Smart people don't get out of high school or college and then just coast the rest of their lives. They look at life as one long learning opportunity. Whether it's reading or taking classes or simply watching the Food Channel for cooking tips, you'll be a better person if you keep the education flowing.

"As humans, we are learning machines," says Kevin Eikenberry, owner of the Indianapolis-based learning consulting company The Eikenberry Group. "We are most alive and functioning closest to our potential when we are learning, adapting, adjusting and finding new ways, approaches and techniques to improve our lives (or the lives of others) in some way."

According to Eikenberry, continuous learners:

1. **Have a beginner's mind-set.** If you approach something as an expert, you will learn nothing because experts want confirmation and validation of what they already know. Beginners, on the other hand, look constantly for a new tidbit, another way to expand on their current expertise. They know that only with a beginner's mind can they benefit from a learning opportunity.

2. **Make connections.** Continuous learners think about what they have learned in one part of their life and how it relates to and connects with challenges, problems, opportunities and situations that occur in other parts of their life.

3. **Are flexible and adaptable.** Learning requires change, so continuous learners realize that they must be willing to adapt and change if they want to grow.

4. **Are always learning something.** Continuous learners learn new things "just because." Maybe they've always wanted to play the guitar, so they take lessons. They want to ride a unicycle, so they try it. They learn how to quilt. They learn a new language. They realize that their brains are like muscles: The more they exercise them the stronger they will be.

5. **Are continuously curious.** One of the most powerful learning questions we use is "Why?" Continuous learners remain curious about people, places, important and mundane things as well. By cultivating their curiosity they are adding to their knowledge and perspective, while exercising an important part of their learning brain at the same time.

6. **Learn in multiple ways.** In school we learned in a relatively limited number of ways, which unfortunately leaves some people with a limited view of learning. Continuous learners know that they can learn by reading, by listening, by trying, through others, with a mentor and more.

7. **Teach others.** Something happens when you teach someone something—you suddenly understand it better yourself. Continuous learners teach others both to help the other person and because they know it helps them deepen their mastery of their own learning.

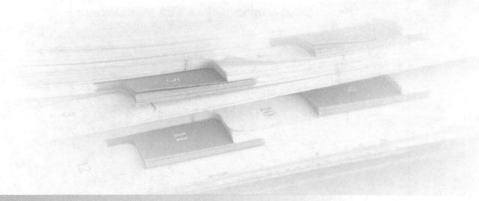

"Courage and perseverance have a magical talisman, before which difficulties disappear and obstacles vanish into air."

— *John Quincy Adams*

Invest in Yourself
(Sometimes It Really *Is* All About You)

My friend Samantha was an executive at a mid-sized Phoenix-based advertising agency when she chanced upon a strategy that changed her life. It actually had nothing to do with business (like "eat lunch with your boss" or "find the right mentor"). But it had a profound effect on her ability to stay focused on making her career into something that was interesting and worthwhile for her. Simply put, Samantha gave herself time off.

Her time off, however, wasn't spent in idle relaxation. Each month, for one day, Samantha would invest in something that would improve her life. One month, for example, she took a course in hip-hop dancing. Another month, she packed a picnic lunch and hiked into the McDowell Mountains. Yet another time, she got together with a few friends for a round of golf and lunch. All told, Samantha's strategy breathed new life into her and helped her face the rest of her month with renewed energy.

What could you do that would be an investment in you? Think about what gives you peace, what makes you happy, what things reenergize you. At the end of each "investment day," make notes about what you did and how you felt afterward. Next year, be sure you make time for those activities that were the most successful.

Get Over Yourself
(Self-absorption Isn't Pretty)

You might think there's a fine line between taking care of yourself and wallowing in your own special "you-ness." Maybe it's a matter of degree, but you'll know it when you're doing it. When you can't stop thinking and talking about yourself and your needs and your fears and your house and your car and your plans, then you've stepped over the line. You've become self-absorbed.

Self-absorbed people generally don't listen well to others because they're too busy thinking about themselves. They're selfish and petty and not that much fun to be around. If this sounds a bit too familiar, then it's time to take steps to get outside yourself. Make a mental adjustment by spending time every day attending to the interests of others. They'll appreciate it, and ultimately, so will you.

> *"Everybody gets so much information all day long*
> *that they lose their common sense."*
>
> — *Gertrude Stein*

Schedule Rest Periods
(Get Down With Down Time)

Perhaps an investment in yourself would be to just rest. After all, most of us get so overbooked that it's difficult sometimes to simply relax. But just as a good night's sleep makes everything look better the next day, so does a healthy bout of rest—whether you're asleep or not.

What would happen if you decided not to attend that Friday night party? How would people react if you chose to skip the Saturday morning soccer practice? What might befall you if you fell asleep at 10 rather than midnight?

Experts say you might be better off. "It amazes me that contemporary work and social culture glorifies sleeplessness in the way we once glorified people who could hold their liquor," says Dr. Charles Czeisler, a sleep studies expert at Harvard Medical School. In an October 2006 article in the *Harvard Business Review*, Czeisler goes on to say that "like a drunk, a person who is sleep-deprived has no idea how functionally impaired he or she truly is."

When you rest, you give your mind time to regenerate and repair. Sleep helps your body recover from all the work you do while you're awake, and some experts even believe that sleep helps form memories. If you fight that gnawing voice that tells you to rest, consider that eight out of ten people in a 2001 National Sleep Foundation survey said they would sleep more if they knew it would improve their health and memory.

Now you know.

> *"Everywhere I have sought rest and not found it, except sitting in a corner by myself with a little book."*
>
> — *Thomas Kempis*

Have Fun
(Get Serious About Your Sense of Humor)

Did you know that only 15 percent of employees are fired because they can't do their jobs? In a survey by Robert Half International, the international staffing firm found that a whopping 85 percent of workers are let go because of their inability to get along with their fellow employees. When asked about the qualities of an effective employee, supervisors and human relations people said that humor is one of the choice attributes of a desired employee.

Why has humor become such an important asset in the workplace? Because a strong sense of humor facilitates communication, builds relationships, reduces stress and provides perspective. In a nutshell, humor makes working a lot more fun.

> "Humor is the great thing, the saving thing. The minute it crops up, all our irritations and resentments slip away and a sunny spirit takes their place."
>
> — Mark Twain

How do you develop your sense of humor? We're not talking about the ability to crack jokes here, because there are few people who are really good at that—and while it might be fun, it's not even necessary. But the ability to have fun at work and in your life comes from three simple places:

1. You have to see the positive side of serious or sometimes negative situations. If you can think positively about things, then you're close to seeing the funny side.

2. You should have a good sense of irony. Some of the best stand-up comics capitalize on hilarious headlines, grammatical errors and other media mistakes. The ability to enjoy puns, plays on words or double-entendres demonstrates a good sense of humor.

3. And last, but maybe most important, you should never take yourself too seriously. Laugh at your own mistakes, find an inside joke about yourself and share it with those who will appreciate it. The ability to laugh at yourself is the mark of a person with a great sense of humor.

Chapter 5:
How You Deal With Others

In 1936, Dale Carnegie wrote a bestselling book that still resonates today. Released in the midst of the Great Depression, *How to Win Friends and Influence People* created a stir because of the book's concise advice to be nice. Born a poor farmer's son in Missouri, Carnegie based his premise on his years of sales experience, during which he continually advanced to the top of every company he worked for.

In a nutshell, Carnegie believed that it's possible to change other people's behavior by changing one's reaction to them. His six ways to make people like you—which, by the way, haven't gone stale, even though they're 80 years old—go like this:

1. Become genuinely interested in other people

2. Smile

3. Remember that a person's name is to that person the sweetest and most important sound in any language

4. Be a good listener. Encourage others to talk about themselves.

5. Talk in terms of the other person's interests

6. Make the other person feel important—and do it sincerely

Why is it so important to get along with others—and to help others bring out the best in themselves? Because when you reach outside yourself to help others, or to get along better with them, then you've actually done something for both of you. Since we're all in this together, doesn't it make sense that you win when others win?

"I think a hero is an ordinary individual who finds strength to persevere and endure in spite of overwhelming obstacles."

— Christopher Reeve

Make Someone Else Feel Good (It's Nice to Be Nice)

Whether you're a CEO or a secretary, you have powerful reasons to be thoughtful of others. You can give a compliment, send a birthday card, do an unasked-for favor, drop a note of encouragement or phone a friend. Whatever you do, you'll find the benefits to you will probably outweigh the benefits to the other person. "One of the first real-life lessons my parents taught me when I was a child is perhaps the most basic of all," writes Richard Carlson in *Don't Sweat the Small Stuff at Work*. "If you want to feel good about yourself, make someone else feel good! It really is that simple."

What are some small ways to start being more thoughtful?

- Look around you at the odd jobs others are doing, then help them by taking over for a day, a week or forever
- Keep a master list of birthdays and a file of cards that you can send at a moment's notice. Then write a caring note on each before mailing.
- Try to give one unsolicited compliment every day. Make sure it's genuine and sincere.
- Ask what you can do to help, rather than waiting to be told. You might even suggest ways you can pitch in.

And don't forget about making someone else feel good in a global way. Companies that thoughtfully put their employees and customers first deserve a pat on the back; let them know you appreciate what they're doing.

> *"A strong nation, like a strong person, can afford to be gentle, firm, thoughtful and restrained."*
>
> — *Jimmy Carter*

Be Constructive in Your Criticism (and in Your Praise)

Beverly was my first real boss out of college and she gave me the best piece of advice I've ever received. "Don't come to me with a problem," she said, "unless you also have a solution in mind." That tip has served me well, and has also been passed along to everyone I've ever worked with.

What that also means is that you should have some solid ideas to back up any criticism you might want to offer. Rather than saying, "That proposal was really bad," you should be able to provide some ideas on why it was weak and what the proposal writer might do to improve it. Don't just tell your boss, "I don't like that new guy you want to hire." Be ready to constructively tell him/her why.

And when your criticism is directed at an individual, make sure you lead with something positive. "I really liked the overall tone of this letter," you might say, "but I think we need to work a bit more on the bullet points." You'll find that being constructive will get the job done faster and better—and also preserve the working relationship.

> *"If your success is not on your own terms, if it looks good to the world but does not feel good in your heart, it is not success at all."*
>
> — *Anna Quindlen*

What about praise? Parenting experts make a good point when they urge moms and dads to be specific and direct in their praise. Instead of saying "Good job!" when a child is learning to read, parents are urged to say something like, "It's great to see you reading out loud to yourself. You remember the information when you hear yourself read." This helps children know what they're doing right so that they can repeat the behavior.

It's not so different with adults. Grown-ups want to know specifically what they're doing right, too, and they strive to repeat successful behavior. This is true in boss-employee associations, in romantic relationships and among friends. So when you have something nice to say, be direct and specific.

Manage Your Boss (and Be Managed Well)

Even though the pecking order is established (and you report to your boss), you still have a two-way relationship. And though your job description probably lays out your work responsibilities fairly clearly, you can get along with your supervisor in ways that aren't listed in any employee manual. What might those be? Here are some suggestions, for starters:

Do

- Be professional at all times
- Observe when your boss is in a good mood and act on it
- Inquire about your boss's personal life in a general, caring way
- Model your boss's communication and management style
- Take initiative
- Observe what your boss wants to get out of meetings
- Listen to your boss vent
- Carry out tasks your boss values
- Be resourceful
- Make your boss feel comfortable with you
- Supply your boss with the skills he or she needs to run the business
- Follow your boss's lead
- Always make your boss look good

Don't

- Put business on a personal level
- Speak or act when angry
- Be inflexible
- Compete with your boss—support him or her instead
- Pester your boss on what you believe is right
- Be the bearer of bad news unless you also bring advice, a solution or a plan
- Whine or complain to your boss; instead, be a positive change agent
- Sell out the boss or tell stories about him or her
- Out-ego your boss in front of others
- Neglect or forget former bosses
- Overreact to a new boss in a reorganization

"Whoever gossips to you will gossip about you."

—Spanish proverb

Don't Gossip
(Just Say "No" to Loose Lips)

It turns out that Mom was right: "If you can't say something nice, don't say anything at all" is excellent advice for the workplace. You don't want to get a reputation for being the person who's always got a juicy rumor because, soon, no one will trust you with the truth.

What should you do if you hear something that's just too good to keep to yourself? Keep it to yourself anyway! If there's truth to it, then you'll know soon enough. Although knowledge of something that's about to occur may help you to prepare an appropriate reaction, you don't need to spread it around.

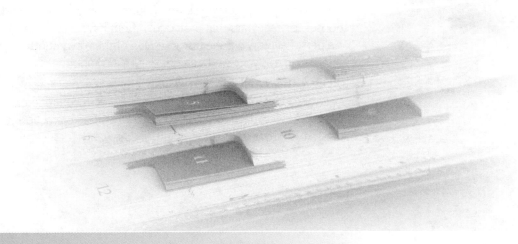

"Live in such a way that you would not be ashamed to sell your parrot to the town gossip."

— Will Rogers

Deal With Difficult People (There Oughta' Be a Law)

Entire books have been written about dealing with difficult people (some with those very words in the title), and if this is a major issue for you, then you should get yourself to the library and check some of them out. Chances are, however, that you'll have some standard issue tough guys in your career, but nothing that spirals into disaster. Rest assured: Everyone gets a difficult person at some point (or points) in their working life.

Although there are all sorts of challenging personality types, Robert McGovern boils it down to three essential types in his book *Bring Your "A" Game*. These, he writes, "can drive the best and brightest people to their wits' end, leaving a wake of stress, dismay and frustration in their path." Here's how McGovern, also the founder of CareerBuilder, summarizes those three types:

- **The Intimidator.** Stern, abrupt and unapproachable, he's got a reputation for being smart but no-nonsense. Rather than exhibiting the classic traits of the secure person—a self-deprecating sense of humor, approachability and empathy—he chooses to erect walls that protect him from having to reveal his weaknesses. This personality style is the office version of the playground bully. He knows he's intimidating everyone and he's perfectly happy about it.

  What are the secrets to working with people like this? Forget about trying to win him over; this guy doesn't want friends. Instead, focus your energies on earning his respect. Be prepared for meetings and virtually every other interaction with him. Do your research, jot down discussion points and be ready.

- **The Obstructionist.** She seems to exist for one reason: To make sure things don't happen. You've got a clear vision in your mind of what needs to be done, and she's seemingly there as your biggest roadblock. She asserts her ability to block things, and people become disgruntled, thus giving her what she wants—the feeling of position, power and relevance.

  What can you do? Don't worry about being right; keep your eye on your objective, which is to get what you need to succeed. Forget about demanding; instead, try to be understanding of her job and difficulties. A little empathy will go a long way with this personality type.

- **Mr. Ambition.** The term "blind ambition" describes a person who is so focused on his goal that he can't see the harm he's causing others. Mr. Ambition will take credit for other people's work, he'll maneuver behind your back and at your expense and he'll try hard not to let the truth get in the way of his version of his accomplishments.

  What can you do? First off, don't let him get to you; there's a strong probability that higher-ups know what's going on. Secondly, you might kindly point out that others should get equal time. Third, consider saying something to your boss in a constructive, problem-solving manner.

"Courage is fear that has said its prayers."

— *Dorothy Bernard*

Deal With Unethical People (When There Is a Law)

Sometimes you may come up against people or behavior that's not just difficult, but downright unethical or, even, illegal. Whether it's cooking the books or nipping paper clips, unethical behavior is wrong, and you'll have to decide how to handle what you know or are being asked to do. Sometimes, your decision can change the course of your career.

Before you act on anything, make sure you understand company policy. What's unethical in one situation may be less so in another. Be certain you understand the impact on the company. Is what the person is doing detrimental to the organization? Will it negatively affect the bottom line? Will it harm the company's reputation or its customers? If you can't make these assessments yourself, then ask a trusted mentor or other person to help.

If you've decided that you must report the ethical breach, then choose carefully whom to tell. A trusted senior manager or the head of human resources may be the best option. In the event that they won't listen or act, then decide whether you need to go outside the company with your information or, ultimately, whether you should find a new place of employment.

"To live a creative life, we must lose our fear of being wrong."

— *Joseph Chilton Pearce*

Find a Role Model
(Be a Role Model)

In the rush to focus on the role of mentors these days, many people forget that role models are just as crucial. They come in so many forms and can teach us so many different things. We watch how they respond to situations, we study how they live their lives, we notice the way they treat others. Those who are especially adept at a variety of situations become life's most valuable role models.

Think about your role models. Maybe your mom and dad modeled good parenting skills. Perhaps your first boss demonstrated grace under fire. Maybe a teacher showed you how to explain complicated things clearly and humorously. Whoever you consider your life's coaches comprise a valuable virtual school for you.

Likewise, you can be (and probably are already, whether you know it or not) a role model for others. People watch how you behave and learn from it, for good *and* bad. Think about this when you're tempted to drink heavily at an office party (you'll be a negative role model) or when you refuse to participate in office gossip (positive role model). Your friends, co-workers and bosses aren't just looking at you—they're learning, too.

"Trouble is only opportunity in work clothes."

— *Henry J. Kaiser*

Stay Calm
(Don't Tie Your Stomach Up in Knots)

"We only have five minutes until the meeting starts, and I don't have all the copies made!"

"There's a customer on line two who's furious!"

"Can't anybody help me get this project finished!"

Notice how all these sentences end with an exclamation point? Even the one that's really a question! You can hear the frustration and the sense of disaster in each one and you can probably relate to it, because fear and desperation are common in the workplace. It doesn't have to be that way, and if you're the one who can stay calm in a choppy sea of stress, then you'll be far ahead of everyone who's paddling like crazy for a shore that's right in front of them.

Sure, you'll have times when stress and nervousness are appropriate. But why get worked up about it? Does it resolve the situation—or even help? Better to be the calm port in the storm and know that whatever is getting everyone riled up will surely pass, whether you join in or not. Try asking yourself, "Will this matter in five years—or even next week?" If not, then it's not really worth getting worked up over, is it?

Make the Best of Every Job
(Even if You Think It's Boring)

In *Don't Sweat the Small Stuff at Work*, Richard Carlson tells a very enlightening story that speaks well to the idea that your job is what you make of it. It goes like this:

> Two bricklayers were interviewed by a reporter. The reporter asked the first worker how he spent his day. He replied in a resentful tone, "I spend hours in the hot sun picking up these stupid bricks and putting them on top of each other. Leave me alone."

> The reporter turned to the second worker and asked the same question. His response was quite different. He said in a grateful, enthusiastic tone, "I take these simple bricks and turn them into beautiful structures. Without people like me, there would be no buildings and no economy."

Sometimes people get the idea that what they're doing is boring, uncreative or even dumb. Sometimes they're right (I'm thinking of the job I had flipping burgers, for example). But what you make of it can make all the difference for you and your peace of mind. You can be miserable and the days will be long and repetitive and your health will probably suffer. Or you can be upbeat and hopeful and do the best job you can do.

That kind of attitude can also lead you right out of that job and into another one. After all, the employee with a positive, can-do attitude is much more likely to attract the attention of others in a position to hire. In addition, your positive attitude will make life more pleasant for everyone around, which helps them succeed, too.

"Having once decided to achieve a certain task, achieve it at all costs of tedium and distaste. The gain in self-confidence of having accomplished a tiresome labor is immense."

— Arnold Bennett

Admit Responsibility
(You're in Charge of Your Reaction)

Sometimes it's hard to be accountable for mistakes and missteps. But people who can't accept their own role in the events of their lives are bound to feel angry and victimized. It's when you acknowledge your own accountability that you're most likely to be able to learn and grow and put things behind you.

Consider this chart adapted from *The Valuable Office Professional*. In it, author Michelle Burke illustrates the difference between confidently responding to events and letting events determine your reaction.

When we're accountable, we're shaping events …

- We believe that we are 100 percent responsible for the various events in our lives (both positive and negative)
- We recognize our own contribution to positive and negative events in our lives
- We appreciate events we see as as positive. We strive to create them recurrently.
- We examine negative events to understand our contribution and take action to create more positive events in the future

When we're unaccountable, we're being stopped by events …

- We believe that events in our lives just happen to us
- We don't recognize or acknowledge our own contribution to positive and negative events
- We attribute events to persons or things beyond our control:
  — We consider ourselves lucky when positive events happen and give credit to others
  — We play victim when negative events happen; we blame people or things

So, are you an actor or a reactor? Even the mail room clerks or lunch staff or office gardeners—who may seem to be far down the corporate ladder—must decide how to respond to the events of their lives. You can choose, too.

Use Respect
(and Keep the Peace)

Angela's children were students at a well-respected parochial school in Chicago, and when she signed onto the Parent-Teacher Association's executive committee she assumed the group would embody those religious values. But she quickly found out that the bickering and in-fighting amongst the PTA members rivaled what you might find among inner-city high school students—not the adults they were supposed to be. Where, she wondered, was the respect and moral compass that should have been guiding the group's actions?

Every group has its own dynamics, and sometimes they can be toxic. But there are ways of dealing with these kinds of situations, short of finding the nearest exit. In fact, Angela learned two important things during her year on the PTA, and they apply equally well to any occasion, whether it's business or personal. "Never get in the middle of a disagreement between two people," says Angela, who's also a part-time paralegal, "and never gossip if a third person who's not there will be hurt in any way."

Simply thinking about how other people will react to what you say and do goes a long way toward success in any situation. Respect other people's feelings with your words and actions and the world will smile down on you.

See the Good in Everyone (Put on a Positive Spin)

You don't have to be a Pollyanna about it, but why not try viewing all your colleagues through a positive prism? There's something to be said for noticing the good things about someone, then trying to compliment them on that trait once a week.

Say one of your co-workers is really good at schmoozing. The next time you're at a departmental meeting and he works the room with his usual finesse, you can tell him afterwards, "I really admire the way it's so easy for you to talk to everyone. That's a valuable skill." When another colleague, who's adept at alphabetizing, gets the work done especially quickly, try telling him, "I really admire how fast you can put those in order. That's a great talent."

When you can look generously at the people around you, you'll be a lot closer to being generous with yourself. And your actions will encourage others to also view the world and its inhabitants more positively.

Be Careful What You Share (Too Much Information!)

Which would you share? Details about your messy divorce or stories about your daughter's piano recital? How your pap smear went last week or your latest escapade on the softball field? While it's good to share yourself with your co-workers, you must decide how far is too far when it comes to personal information.

"When is personal information too much information to share?" writes Kathleen Archambeau in *Climbing the Corporate Ladder in High Heels*. "It is a fine line between revelation and exhibitionism. Revelation provokes greater understanding and closeness. Exhibitionism attracts voyeurs. Voyeur-based interest is laden with judgment, derision, gossip and mean-spirited intent."

So how to decide? Says Archambeau: "One rule of thumb is that if you don't want the information posted on the company bulletin board outside the cafeteria, don't tell anyone at work."

Focus on the Sameness
(Look Past the Differences)

Not long ago, I went to meeting where I didn't know anyone. I started chatting with a young woman who was tall and exotic-looking. At first, I thought we probably would have nothing in common. As we talked, however, we realized that we'd gone to the same university, we have children in the same school and she was living next door to my dad's old house. It gave us a common ground that made the rest of the meeting more enjoyable— and resulted in a contact that we've maintained.

It's fun to connect with someone. But you have to be willing to share yourself in order to find those similarities that will create a bond. With your co-workers, be ready to tell a funny story about yourself or reveal an amusing observation. With your boss, commiserate when her baby keeps her up all night or his car breaks down. With your friends, remember aloud what it was like to have a bad hair day or a rotten review.

Remember that you don't want to share inappropriate information, but rather something which helps you find a common ground. In the end we're all really more alike than different anyway. By keeping that in mind you can make connections that will serve you in every setting.

Be Kind (to Yourself and Others)

Put another way: Give yourself and others a break. Don't be too critical or unforgiving. When you make a mistake, own up to it and move on. Don't get worked up about the small stuff because, at the end of the day, it doesn't really matter. Be kind. Be thoughtful. And be the best you can be. Others will follow suit.

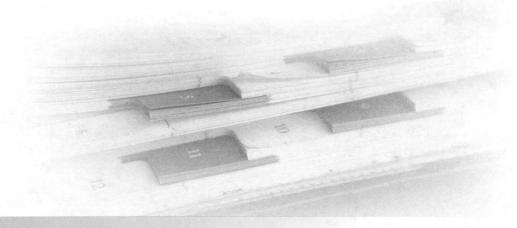

"Don't be discouraged by a failure. It can be a positive experience. Failure is, in a sense, the highway to success, inasmuch as every discovery of what is false leads us to seek earnestly after what is true, and every fresh experience points out some form of error which we shall afterwards carefully avoid."

— John Keats

Notes

Notes

Notes

Notes

Notes